You Are Beautiful

WRITTEN BY

Mary Tabitha Deutsch

ILLUSTRATED BY

Kate Solenova

Copyright © 2021

Mary Tabitha Deutsch

Performance Publishing Group

McKinney, TX

All Worldwide Rights Reserved.
All rights reserved. No part of this publication may be reproduced, stored in a retrieval system or transmitted, in any form or by any means, electronic, mechanical, recorded, photocopied, or otherwise, without the prior written permission of the copyright owner, except by a reviewer who may quote brief passages in a review.

ISBN: 978-1-946629-80-7

Lovingly dedicated to Nayeli Hall, Abigail Rautio, Kaia Hall,
and Henry Rautio.
... and to anyone who has ever felt different. You are loved.

A very special thank you to Joe Schaefer for all of his love, support, and patience, and for being a voice of encouragement and reason through the publication process and in life.

To my siblings who have been a lifelong influence: Sarah, I have always looked up to you and wanted your approval. You make me better. Rachel, I have always wished I was there for you more. You make me vulnerable and you soften my heart. Paul, I have always felt the need to teach and protect you. You make me laugh and remember to live in the present.

Finally, a big thank you to of the people at Performance Publishing, especially Michelle Prince, Ana Borlescu, and Kate Solenova. Without your help, guidance, and patience through every edit, this book would not exist. I am grateful for you all!

A note to the adult reader:

This book was written late one night as I was lying in bed and drifting off to sleep. I had just returned from a book conference where I experienced some life-changing, eye-opening moments. A weekend surrounded by people who were hungry for personal growth and development and who were filled up by encouraging and helping others.

I spent a lot of time that weekend thinking about my childhood and about my nieces. Although I don't have children of my own, I hold such a special place in my heart for the world's youth. I often think about how they encounter challenges, embrace differences, and how so many of us have formed our beliefs and opinions based on the examples that were set before us.

That night as I lay in bed thinking about my nieces, I wondered if they would know that they are loved and beautiful no matter what. I wonder how many times children need to be reminded of this as they grow into teens and young adults ... and how many of us in adulthood need this reminder as well.

My desire is that the children and adults reading this book will have the opportunity to think about and discuss what it means to be different without judgment or fear. I imagine the child reading or being read to might ask questions about the pictures they see and the words they read. There are so many people in the world, and although I wasn't able to show all of the ways we can be unique, my goal was to recognize a few of these physical distinctions in the characters throughout this book.

I hope that our differences will invite questions and understanding rather than assumptions and opposition. I pray the children of the world may grow up to treat others with dignity and respect and that all of us may celebrate our individuality. At the end of the book, there's a note to the kids. Please take a moment to read it and reflect on it with your children.

From your lovely cheesy smile to your goofy little laugh,

You are beautiful, my darling, always remember that!

Your heart is pure. You have no fear.

You're strong and smart and kind.

You're spunky and you're crazy,
and you have a creative mind!

You dance around, prance and bound,

wild, careless, and free.

You're as beautiful as an angel, everyone can see!

You build in the sand, dirty your hands.

You're a messy little one;

But however you play, you're loved anyway,

So go on, and have some fun!

You might enjoy sports, music, or games;

whatever you like, you're loved just the same.

Maybe you like to write or draw.

Be proud of your talents. Always stand tall!

Your ears, your tears, your fears -

both big and small,

Look inside your pretty soul

for the courage to be you!

You can change the world and be yourself,

and you will make mistakes.

But don't you fret and don't regret;

you'll have so many takes!

Be true to you, through and through,

and you'll be most happy then.

You're beautiful-inside and out-
because beauty comes from within!

A message to the child reading this book:

Everyone has physical features (the way we look) and personality traits (the way we act and speak) that are unlike anyone else. We are born with some, yet others will change based on the people we meet, things we do, places we go, and so on. These are called experiences. Throughout your whole life, you will meet people that look or think differently than you do! No two of us are exactly alike. That's what makes each of us special! I want you to know that you are beautiful just as you are, inside and out.

Think of a few ways that you are different from other people. Now, let's celebrate your differences and how beautiful you are! Write down some of the ways that you are unique, special, and different from others.

_____
_____
_____
_____

Now that you know it's okay to be different and unique, if you are beautiful just as you are, doesn't it make sense that other people are beautiful and special just as they are too? Try to think of ways that other people are different. Try to think of times when you might have thought someone was weird because they weren't like you. Think of strangers you have met, your friends, neighbors, schoolmates, and even people in your family. Write down ways that other people are different than you are. (If you are having trouble, flip back through the book and see if you can find some examples.)

_____
_____
_____
_____

Remember that you are special and loved, and remember to show other people that they are special and loved, especially when they are different from you. We all make this world a very special place to live!

www.ingramcontent.com/pod-product-compliance
Lightning Source LLC
Chambersburg PA
CBHW061604170426
43196CB00039B/2971